The Love of DOGS

Wendy Boorer John Holmes
Margaret Osborne Mary Roslin-Williams
Alan Hitchins Howard Loxton

The Love of DOGS

OCTOPUS Octopus Books

First published 1974 by
Octopus Books Limited
59 Grosvenor Street, London W1

ISBN 0 7064 0353 3

Distributed in USA by
Crescent Books
a division of Crown Publishers Inc
419 Park Avenue South
New York, N.Y. 10016

Distributed in Australia by
Rigby Limited
30 North Terrace, Kent Town
Adelaide, South Australia 5067

Produced by Mandarin Publishers Limited
14 Westlands Road, Quarry Bay, Hong Kong

Printed in Hong Kong

Contents

The faithful friend

Howard Loxton

WE ALWAYS think of our dogs as our friends, we expect them to stand by us, to be understanding when we are down and to put our interests above all others. In return we allow them to share our lives and join in our fun: but only when we say so. Obedience is all. This is more than we would expect of any other creature yet, with few exceptions, when there are instances of real cruelty, the dog is tail-wagging happy and loves pleasing us.

One might imagine that this was a situation contrived by man to give himself a willing slave and courtier, but it seems likely that it was originally the dog who saw the advantage in throwing in his lot with human beings. Probably wild dogs first attached themselves to man by scavenging around his camp, or outside his cave, and perhaps man first became aware of dogs' usefulness when he realized that their barking gave warning of the approach of strangers or other animals. Dogs offered no threat to man and their presence was encouraged. They followed men on hunting expeditions, looking for pickings. Then they began to cooperate in bringing down the quarry and shared in the kill.

Dog and man began to trust each other and from the perimeter of the camp the dog moved into a place closer to the fire.

His puppies grew up with man's children as their playfellows, and the dog became the first animal to be domesticated.

As a mutual dependance developed the dog began to identify his group of humans with his canine pack, giving to them his loyalty and his strong instinct for mutual defence. Now man began to have the upper hand. Reared to be dependent upon man, and trained to perform a variety of services for him, the dog developed a need for man's approval and man found a loyalty far greater than he usually met in others.

There are many tales told of dogs' devotion to their masters. One of the earliest recorded actual dogs must be the dog which belonged to Xanthippus, father of the Pericles who led Athens in its golden age. He swam beside his master's galley across the bay of Salamis and was eventually buried at the place thereafter called Cynosema: 'the dog's grave.'

Left: The dog was probably first domesticated in the countries of the Middle East but by the Stone Age had already reached northern Europe. The modern Spitz type, of which this Finnish Spitz is an example, is very like the kind of dog whose remains have been found with those of early man in northern Europe, and a small Spitz was one of the breeds known to the ancient Egyptians and kept by them as a domestic pet.

Right: There is no better example of the mutual trust and friendship that exists between dog and man than the way in which a dog will obey a child and the child in return will have complete confidence in a large, strong animal–here a collie.

At Corinth it is said that 50 guard dogs defended the city from a surprise attack whilst the city's soldiers slept. All were killed but one which roused the garrison who repulsed the attackers. In gratitude the city raised a marble monument in the dogs' memory and granted the survivor a pension and a heavy silver collar.

Probably the best known of Greek dogs is the legendary Argus in Homer's *Odyssey*, a hound who could still recognize the voice and scent of his master after an absence of 20 years. When the wily Odysseus sailed for Troy he left behind a puppy he had reared and trained himself, but which was still too young to have been taken on a hunt. After ten years of war and ten more years of wandering Odysseus returned, disguised by the goddess Athena as an old beggar. The aged Argus was lying, cast out and neglected, on a dunghill outside the palace. He recognized his master when no human did, and tried his best to wag

---

Right: The lives of polar explorers and many other travellers in the Arctic and Antarctic wastes have often depended on the strength and fortitude of husky sled dogs whose deep coats enable them to withstand the rigours of an arctic blizzard. The Siberian Husky is the only official breed to

carry the husky name but the Alaskan Malamute and a variety of 'unofficial' husky types are also used as sled dogs. The Samoyed (above) is another pure bred husky which came from the Siberian Tundra and has a very thick stand off coat with a ruff round the neck. They are now very popular house dogs, particularly in the States, and it is not hard to see why when one sees the puppies.

Above: The wide world still seems a rather intimidating place to this nine week old Jack Russell puppy. If you raise a dog from puppyhood you will have the greatest possible chance to influence its character and development.

Below: This English Springer Spaniel has been off to investigate something that has caught his interest, a rabbit hole perhaps? and hurries to catch up with his master. Dogs like to play an active role in their owner's life but this does not stop them taking time out for their own affairs.

his tail and show his love, although he was too weak to rise and greet Odysseus.

From those ancient times to the present day countless dogs have defended home and property, saved their masters' lives and even tracked down murderers. Some of their stories are told in the pages that follow. The Italian artist Benvenuto Cellini, for instance, tells in his memoirs of the courage and intelligence of his dog, who surprised a jewel thief robbing the shop where Cellini fashioned gold and dealt in gems. Unable to grapple with the man, who was armed with a sword, he tried to rouse the journeyman who simply cursed him and threw stones. Returning to the attack he followed the man into the street and managed to tear off his cloak, but, when the burglar called on passers by to save him from 'a mad dog', he was driven off. However, the dog's intervention had stopped the man from pocketing more than a few trinkets. Some while later the dog suddenly attacked a young man who was being arrested for another robbery. The dog's assault made him drop some packets from the folds of his cloak in which the stolen property was discovered, together with gold, silver, and a ring of Cellini's.

The great and noble are not the only people who bring forth devotion in their pets, as we all know from experience. We can only hope to repay some of the devotion which the dog gives to us personally, and to the service of mankind, by the affection we can return and the care we can take to ensure that he has a happy and healthy life.

Far left: A lively Golden Retriever will need plenty of exercise and will enjoy being taught to retrieve even if he is not to be a gun dog.

Left: The Saint Bernard is the breed most famous for bringing help to humans in distress, although not the only one used as a rescue dog. Kept by the monks of the Hospice du Grand States for hunting cottontail rabbits these guide and rescue dogs have saved the lives of countless travellers in the deep mountain snows – but contrary to romantic belief they do not carry a keg of brandy around their necks. There are rough and smooth coated types of this breed. This is a smooth coated dog.

Left: The Mastiff is a very ancient breed, used as a fighting dog by the Assyrians and Babylonians. It can be a very powerful dog as a valet to Sir Henry Lee discovered in the sixteenth century. Sir Henry kept a Mastiff, called Bevis, as a guard dog. He gave the animal little attention yet one evening Bevis insisted on following Sir Henry and his valet to his master's chamber and when he was turned away made such a fuss that he was eventually permitted to sleep beneath the bed. In the middle of the night an intruder came into the room. As Sir Henry woke he saw the dog pin the man to the floor. It was the valet, who later confessed that he had proposed to kill his master and rob the house.

Right: The loyal and intelligent Dalmatian has performed many tasks. At different times it has been a sportsman's dog, a watchdog, a draught dog, a war dog, a shepherd and a performing dog. Now it is a very popular pet, but this elegant dog's pose is a reminder of the days when the Dalmatian would trot between the wheels of an English aristocrat's carriage or even point the way, ahead of the leading horse, turning every outing into a stately procession.

Left: The Welsh prince Llewelyn ap Iorweth, returning to his camp, found his dog Gelert covered with blood and his tent in chaos. There was no sign of the baby prince he had left there and Llewelyn, suspecting that Gelert had killed his child, flew into a towering rage and flung his spear at the dog. Then, beneath the upturned cradle of the child he found the body of a huge wolf and the baby still unharmed. The faithful and courageous dog had killed the wolf and saved the child and had been repaid by being killed himself. Filled with remorse Llewelyn mourned the dog, and buried him in the valley which still bears the name Beddgelert. A romantic nineteenth century version of the story describes Gelert as a greyhound but it seems more likely that if the legend is true it was a dog more like this present day Irish Wolfhound.

Sheep and cattle dogs

Margaret Osborne

THERE ARE over 70 different types of sheep and cattle herding dogs and more than half of these are found in Europe alone. Britain itself has nine pedigree herding breeds, seven of them recognized by the Kennel Club, (the Border and Welsh Collies, although unrecognized by them, have stud books which are zealously guarded by the International Sheepdog Society). Australia, South Amercia, Africa and the Middle East all have their own herding dogs but, suprisingly, North America does not have an indigenous breed.

Sheepdogs, world wide, vary enormously in type, each being adapted to suit the kind of work expected of it and the type of terrain on which it has to perform. In Poland, for instance, there is the Tatra Mountain Sheepdog, reaching at least 28 inches at the shoulder, while the Little Sheepdog of the Polish valleys attains a height of a mere 12 inches.

In most cases sheep and herding dogs have a treble role to perform: they help their master tend the flock or herd, act as guard to the homestead and the family and in some parts of the world, even today, ward off wolves and other large predators. As a result the majority of the herding breeds are very sweet tempered, reliable and trustworthy towards their owners and the family, but at the same time make it clear that they are ready to protect the flock, home and family to the death if necessary. On a farm they will often be an 'all-purpose' dog, even to the extent of being gundog, retriever and poacher in addition to their other duties.

The character of the true sheepdog, no matter what his nationality, makes him quite exceptional. I have never encountered any of the herding breeds which were not highly intelligent, sensible and sensitive, as well as having an innate desire to please. Their brains seem to function and reason in almost the same way as our own. Sheepdogs are strongly telepathic, much more so than the other breeds. They have a strong sense of possession and a great sense of right and wrong—especially when it is *we* who are right or wrong! They are extremely sensitive to our moods and their understanding of them is quite uncanny.

Whether the dog is at its daily work, training to compete for trials or just being a family pet his mission in life is to meet with approval, and he goes about his task of trying to please in an unobtrusive manner. If a dog is kept as a pet and cannot carry out his natural duties it is essential to help him to fulfil himself. He must

Left: Border Collie; the most familiar sight behind a flock of sheep, and a true working dog not really suitable for domestic life.

Right: A Kelpie, or Australian Collie, at work controlling the unloading of sheep from a truck. One of the founders of this breed won the first Australian sheepdog trials in 1872. Now some 80,000 Kelpies are working on the sheep stations of the continent.

This page: In these pictures, taken at a Sheepdog Trial at Longshaw in Britain, a Border Collie is seen gathering sheep from a location out of sight when the instruction was given him, and then on instructions given by calls or hand signals driving them between a pair of gates. He next collects a further pair of sheep, brings them to where the first group are and drives the whole flock into the fenced enclosure.

Far right: An Australian sheepdog with his flock. Sheepdogs learn to respond to an elaborate system of commands, usually given by whistles, arm signals or calls or a combination of signals and calls. The method depends upon the terrain in which shepherd and dog are working; and on the whole dogs are trained to recognize sharp, clear whistles which carry well and are easily differentiated particularly when they will be working out of sight of the shepherd.

never be bereft of human companionship, for his fertile mind will go to seed and he will become sad, maybe even untrustworthy. An intelligent dog who is bored is often a naughty dog.

If you have never watched these dogs in difficult terrain or in sheepdog trials you cannot fully appreciate what they can do. Their brilliance has to be seen to be believed. These are not dogs trained by rote. They respond to their master's commands yet use their own brains too. In mountainous country the dog is often out of sight of his master. He *must* use his own intelligence, not just instinct, and solve many difficult problems for himself.

Herding breeds do not all work alike. Sheepdogs working in the plains may lope along hour after hour while others, who must be smaller and more nimble, tend their charges among mountain crags and gullies. All must be trained, but each must also have a tremendous amount of inherited ability and they are often trained as much by their parents as their masters. Putting a young pup with a fully trained adult is a good way to ensure that the pup will have a valuable lesson. Many thousands of years before men began holding dog shows selection was being carried out, probably unconsciously, for the best working dog: the dog with the greatest intelligence and the best suited, physically, for the climate and terrain in which it has to work. Natural selection has played a major part over the centuries, the old law of the survival of the fittest does not mean just the survival of the healthiest but also the most intelligent, at times even the craftiest. That intelligence is needed to understand the complex training with which they are often faced.

A man with a clever dog can handle with the utmost efficiency large flocks and herds which could not possibly be handled by several men without a dog's aid. In these days of mechanized farming the shepherding breeds are happily one group of animals which can never be superceded by machine.

The first Sheepdog Trials in Britain were held in October 1873 in Wales and continued annually, with increases each year both in attendance and the number of competitors. In 1876 the first trials were held in England, and Scotland

Left: A young sheepdog meets his first lamb. The herding instinct is usually so strong that a young puppy will attempt to herd although completely untrained. Scotch Border and Welsh Collies should never really be kept solely as pets as they will be unhappy if left to their own devices and their brains left unused and they have no job to do. The herding and keeping of sheep gives the dog a deep sense of property, helpfulness and loyalty and this inherent instinct will find an outlet in everyday life if he is deprived of his natural work.

Below: The Briard has been used with both sheep and cattle and during the two World Wars was used by the French Army for carrying ammunition, for sentry duty and Red Cross work. As well as driving the flocks to pasture this French breed will also hold a hundred or more head of sheep in an unfenced area designated by a wave of the shepherd's hand. Here and only here, will the sheep be allowed to graze until the shepherd returns, often several hours later.

followed suit in the same year. Six years after the first trials Queen Victoria witnessed a private trial at Bala and this led to the Bala Trials becoming the most important of the annual competitions. Interest in the trials gradually increased until the First World War, when there was a break, but after this they picked up again and not only spread throughout Britain but became increasingly popular in all English speaking countries. Trials throughout the world are now held under the rules of the International Sheepdog Society, as they are in Britain.

The herding breeds are not confined to dogs which work sheep and cattle. In many parts of the world dogs work with goats, pigs, reindeer and other animals. In fact the true pastoral breeds are dogs of enormous adaptability and as well as efficiently carrying out their natural work they can be trained to do very different things, although they are happiest using their strong herding instinct.

Right: The Border Collie is the most common working sheepdog breed but it is not recognized by the English Kennel Club. In Australia and New Zealand, where this champion was photographed holding a group of sheep under the control of his steady eye, it has been recognized by the national Kennel Clubs.

Left: The Rottweiller was probably originally bred for hunting boars but for many centuries it was known as a hardworking cattle dog. This German breed, named after a town in Wurttemberg, had to double as guard dog and drover and would often carry its master's purse around its neck to keep it safe from robbers. When cattle were no longer driven along the road to market it found a new role as a draught dog and later was recruited for duty with the police.

Right: European sheepdogs range through 40 varieties from this big Pyrenean Mountain Dog, which stands over 30 inches at the shoulder, to the little Puli of Hungary. Many of them are large, highly intelligent animals suited to a hardworking outdoor life and for this reason are little known to domestic dog lovers. The Pyrenean has become a favourite pet, however, which has not always been to its advantage and at one stage a 'rescue' service was started to rehouse the puppies that had been bought by people unable to house, feed or exercise such a large dog.

Left: Corgis, although now largely kept as pets, were originally cattle dogs in South Wales. Small and nimble, they could snap at the cattle's heels to keep them on the move yet avoid their kicks. There are now two recognized breeds, the Cardigan and the Pembroke. The latter may have had a different origin from the Cardigan and have been taken to Wales by Flemish weavers about the year 1100, but was a working dog undertaking the same tasks. The Pembroke has a blunter nose and its tail is usually docked. The breed attained great popularity when taken up by King George VI and his family.

Right: The Schnauzer is another German breed that earned its living as a cattle dog but it is now known as a guard and companion dog. There are three different sizes of which this is the miniature variety.

Below: An Old English Sheepdog and her puppy. These dogs are often known as Bobtails from the tradition of docking their tails which originated in the last century when the removal of the tail made the shepherd's dog exempt from tax. A popular breed as a pet, despite the attention their coat requires, this West Country breed is recognized by the Kennel Club as are six other British herding dogs: the Rough and Smooth coated Collies, the Bearded Collie, the Shetland Sheepdog and the Cardigan and Pembrokeshire Corgis.

Above and overleaf: The Smooth and the Rough Collies may once have been separate breeds and it is thought that the smooth coated dog was used largely as a drover, escorting the sheep on their way to market, while the rough coated Collie guarded and herded them upon the hillside. Both types are now much more in evidence on the show bench than as working dogs. In Britain the glamorously coated Rough outnumbers the Smooth by 70 to 1 in Kennel Club registrations and in America the proportion is even higher.

Left: A champion English Bobtail at work with sheep in the United States.

Gundogs

Mary Roslin-Williams

Wʜᴇɴ ᴄʜᴏᴏsɪɴɢ a new puppy many people are attracted to the gundog breeds by their excellent temperaments. Generations of careful breeding for kindness and obedience, willingness and intelligence have produced qualities ideal for the family dog or the gundog. Nevertheless there is a difference in some breeds between the working and the showbred dog, although before becoming a show Champion a gundog must pass certain tests under qualified experts. Retrievers and Spaniels must show that they will hunt and retrieve tenderly (and Spaniels must face covert). Pointers and Setters must show that they have the instinct to

hunt and point. All must show that they are not gunshy, even when off the lead. At the same time it must be remembered that gundogs have been carefully selected for their natural interest in birds and animals. Unless they are given the proper training they will manifest these

---

Right: A Golden Retriever follows close to heel walking up grouse and ptarmigan on a Perthshire hillside.

Below: English breeds are usually used only as pointers or retrievers and many shoots will take out a dog of each kind, but the Continental breeds, such as this Weimaraner, and gundogs in the United States and Canada are often expected to be able to carry out both tasks and they must therefore master both kinds of training. Although individual dogs may put up a superlative performance you cannot expect these breeds in general to do either task as well as a dog bred specifically for the one job. However, general purpose dogs are now coming much more into favour.

Right: An English Springer Spaniel. Spaniels have to flush the bird or rabbit before it is shot. Spaniels are also taught to retrieve and tenderness of mouth and willing delivery to hand is of great importance. Pointers and Setters are not usually taught to retrieve.

instincts in an interest in sheep, deer and poultry. Even a dog that has never seen a gun will have considerable energy, needing space to live and adequate exercise: the big gundogs should not be chosen for life in a small city apartment.

There is nothing more satisfying than working closely with an intelligent, co-operative dog that you have trained yourself. This training starts as soon as you acquire the dog, from the moment that you first put him in his bed and make him stay there. You must get the puppy settled, confident, and at home with you, then you can teach such early commands as sit, stay, heel, not to jump up and to come when called. He must learn and obey that important word 'No'. When he knows all these lessons and his second teeth are fully through the gums you can begin to turn him into a useful worker.

To teach retrieving make a small sausage-shaped dummy from a woollen stocking stuffed with straw and newspaper. Buy a new washing line made of plaited cord from which to cut a length for the dog to wear in training in place of his collar and lead. Make a running noose at one end with a knot to prevent it drawing too tight and choking the dog. At the other end make a knot to stop the cord unravelling or slipping through your fingers. You may be able to buy both dummy and cord ready prepared. Put on the cord and make your dog sit on your left side. Take the dummy and waggle it in front of his nose so that he tries to get it. Then throw the dummy on to open ground in his full view. As he rushes after it drop the cord, turn and *run* back towards his *closed* kennel door, or the back door if his bed is in the house. He will instinctively run after you whereupon intercept him, take the dummy from him gently without pulling and make much of him. He must be made to realize that he has done something ex-

tremely clever and that you are pleased both with him and the dummy. If he gets past you shut his door and get the dummy from him there, praising him in the same way. Repeat this exercise once more and finish his lesson for the day.

From now on, for the rest of his life, he must always be made to sit, for a few seconds at least, before being allowed to go for the dummy. Always send him with the command 'Hie lost' and a forward wave of the hand. Never alter a word of command once taught.

As he progresses vary this lesson by throwing two dummies, one to right and one to left, keeping him sitting. Then with the usual command and wave of the hand towards the dummy you want him to pick, send him to retrieve. Either pick up the second dummy yourself or make him pick up both in the order you require. He must not be allowed to anticipate your wishes but must obey your hand signals. Occasionally keep him sitting for a minute or so to develop his memory and marking ability, forcing

him to note the exact fall and remember the spot accurately. Then he must learn to find an hidden dummy by his nose as well as from your signals. This unseen dummy may puzzle him at first, but if you use hand signals and his usual command he will soon learn that he is often sent for something that he has not seen fall.

It is necessary to teach all breeds of gundog to understand and obey whistle signals. This is done by going through his basic lessons giving the usual signals by raised hand and directional waves but substituting whistles for commands.

To teach him to retrieve from water you need a non-sinkable dummy. Make him sit and then throw the dummy so that it floats just within his depth. Let him get it. Next time throw it a few feet further out so that he just becomes water-borne as he teeters to reach it. The following stage is to throw it just out of his depth so that he has to swim those important few strokes to it and back to the shore. After this he will swim any distance, as he gains confidence that he can swim. At

Above: A Retriever must learn to pick up a bird and carry it without doing it any damage. It must be held gently in the mouth, as this Golden Retriever is holding a duck, without any undue pressure, carried right up to the handler and given up as soon as the sportsman bends to take it from his mouth, but not so quickly that the game falls to the ground. A dog who learns to hold the game tenderly is said to have a 'soft' mouth.

Right: The 'point' is instinctive and the dog must have it in him naturally to freeze when he scents birds on the ground as this Pointer has done. This can be developed or steadied so as to be of maximum use to the sportsman. The dog will indicate the position of the quarry by standing firm with his nose outstretched.

Above: Teaching a Labrador Retriever to respond to whistle signals. He already knows that a raised hand means sit, so instead of the gesture accompanied by the word the trainer uses one short pip to accompany the hand signal. Several quick pips mean 'Come here', a long commanding blast means 'No' and a shortish whistle means 'Look at me for a hand signal' which is followed by a wave to right or left or further away.

Right: Wildfowling with a Spaniel. Retrievers and Spaniels can be trained almost anywhere, in your garden or a public park, but Pointers and Setters require partridge, grouse or quail as a necessary part of their training. Pheasants, rabbits or hares are not suitable for them, although Retrievers and Spaniels deal with the lot. This could be a deciding factor when choosing your breed. Your environment and future shooting requirements must be considered before deciding on the breed of your new puppy.

Above: A Golden Retriever delivers a shot bird. Retrievers and Spaniels must learn to find a shot bird and bring it right into your hand. Their work differs in that Retrievers must walk steadily or sit by your side until the bird has been shot and until they are told to fetch it, while a Spaniel hunts up the bird to the gun.

Left: A young Chesapeake Bay Retriever. Dogs enjoy playing in water and are rarely frightened of it, but always try to give a puppy its first introduction to getting wet at a stream or a pool with a sloping bank and *never* throw a puppy in. If a dog seems over timid wade in yourself and call the puppy to you, for if he has confidence in you he knows that he will be safe. Soon he will be as at home in water as this well trained dog.

31

all times, on land or in water, he must come right up and place the dummy tenderly and willingly in to your out-stretched hand.

Getting a dog used to gunfire requires two people, one to fire the gun and the other – you – to give him his usual 'seen' retrieve. On no account use a rifle. Take a shotgun or a quiet cap pistol, as the sound must not be a sharp loud crack. The 'gun' stands downwind of the dog about 50 yards away. Throw the dummy so that the dog sees it fall. After a few seconds at the 'sit' send him to retrieve. Just as he is reaching out to pick the dummy up the shot is fired. He may hesitate but encourage him to complete the retrieve, then make a great fuss of him. If he is really nervous, increase the distance between puppy and gun.

Once free from gunshyness and good at all his lessons, transfer him from dummy to game by fastening a hen pheasant's wing on to his dummy by strong elastic bands. Once used to that, get hold of a cold but fresh bird or three-quarters grown rabbit to substitute for his winged dummy, thus completing his transfer from dummies to real game. He should now be ready for an easy day in the shooting field and will gain his further experience there.

Retrievers and spaniels are expected to work on all game birds, wildfowl, rabbits and hares once they are fully experienced. Pointers and setters, known as bird-dogs, perform completely different work from retrievers and spaniels, being concerned only with the unshot bird. Their job is to range far and wide in great sweeps, known as 'quartering' the ground. By nose alone they locate the distant birds, immediately freezing to a point which they maintain until the sportsman comes up to them. Both then move slowly towards the birds until they flush and fly away. The shot is fired and, whether hit or miss, the dog must drop to the ground and remain there until put on the cord and led away to start a fresh beat.

Whistle and hand signals may be used to ensure that the dog does not miss any ground when quartering, or to 'drop' a particular area.

Working with pointers and setters is highly specialized and if possible you should already be experienced at working bird dogs before embarking on training your puppy. Then you will know what you are doing, which is vital when so much depends on the handler.

Above: An Irish Water Spaniel. The breed is larger than other Spaniels, has a long tail and a curled coat. It makes an excellent gundog and has a particular aptitude for working in water. In contrast, the Sussex Spaniel (right) was bred to be low to the ground to enable it to push its way through the thick brambles of the southern English county from which it takes its name. It is somewhat slow but very conscientious. It loses favour with sportsmen because it tends to give tongue when working through cover.

Left: An Irish Setter. This handsome bird dog is usually red but may be of the old Red and White colouring, although this is now nearly extinct except in the wildest parts of Ireland. In the right hands the Irish Setter makes a wonderful bird dog. Its fine appearance and pleasant temperament make the breed very popular as a companion dog, but it needs space and plenty of exercise.

Other working dogs

John Holmes

SHEEPDOGS and gundogs are perhaps the largest groups of working dogs but there are many other ways in which dogs work professionally for men. There are records of huge Mastiff type dogs accompanying Babylonian warriors into battle about 2100 BC and this employment was renewed in modern times by the Germans who were the first to experiment with war dogs in about 1870. When the First World War began they had about 6,000 ready for active service. The majority were German Shepherd Dogs (Alsatians) but Dobermans, Rotweillers, Boxers and Airedales were also used. Ironically many of the latter were im-

ported from Britain. It was 1916 before the British Army used war dogs and they proved invaluable. The corps were disbanded after the Armistice.

In World War Two a year passed from the start of hostilities before dogs were used again. Once more their value exceeded all expectations. Patrol dogs were used to give warning of enemy approach and because of their vastly superior sense of smell and hearing they could detect a hidden person when a man would have no idea that he was there. These dogs had to work silently since the slightest whimper might warn the enemy of their whereabouts. They 'pointed' their quar-

ry just as a Pointer indicates a grouse.

Guard dogs were used to protect airfields and ammunition dumps and both the Army and the Air Force continue to use them for this purpose in peacetime. Dogs have been trained as mine detectors and have traced mines buried 10 feet deep in shifting sand. Messenger dogs were also used with conspicuous success. They were trained to work with two handlers, one of whom went out on patrol while the other stayed at base. The dogs carried messages between the two handlers in a special collar. In many cases they worked over ground where a man could easily have been spotted, and,

Left: For military and police work both dog and handler must undergo intensive training and regular refresher courses. The dogs are taught to arrest a man by seizing his arm which is padded to avoid injury. The only time a police dog is ever allowed to attack without being commanded by the handler is if the handler is attacked unexpectedly. When they are used to track the scent of wanted or missing persons police dogs are worked on a very long lead so that they will not be confused by the scent of their handler.

Right: The Bloodhound always seems to have this sad expression in repose. The breed has been used for centuries for tracking criminals and missing persons but recently other breeds have been trained to locate drugs, explosives and firearms. Labrador Retrievers have proved to be the most successful breed for this kind of work.

Right: A German Shepherd Dog with his Police handler in Florida. Since the dog both works and lives with his handler, volunteers for dog patrol work in the United States must produce the written permission of their wives before they can be accepted for training. A trained dog doubles the efficiency of a police patrol, particularly at night, for however highly trained a policeman is in observation his senses cannot match the nose and ears of a dog. The dog not only makes it easier to arrest a cornered wrongdoer, he also deters attacks by troublemakers in dangerous neighbourhoods.

Far right top: The Royal Air Force uses dogs to patrol aerodrome perimeters but this German Shepherd Dog is being put through his paces in an open-day display to entertain the visitors with his skill.

Far right bottom: Husky teams still provide one of the most essential jobs of any working dog today.

of course, they could run faster. Rescue dogs were trained to search for wounded servicemen and, on the home front, to find people buried beneath rubble during the blitz. One Alsatian which I knew very well rescued over 200 people in London. Dogs were also used in Prisoner of War camps both as guards and for tracking escaped prisoners: the number of Allied prisoners caught by German dogs far exceeded the number of German prisoners caught by British dogs.

The vast majority of service dogs today are Alsatians which are easily trained for the work, are about the right size and have coats which are easily cared for yet provide protection from the weather.

The use of dogs for police work was also pioneered in Germany. Most people imagine a police dog as an animal that is ever ready to tear them limb from limb. Police dogs are taught 'man work' and are expected to protect their handlers or to catch a criminal running away but they rarely have the opportunity to do either. The greatest part of a police dog's work is in finding people or clues to their whereabouts. These people may be dangerous criminals, escaped lunatics or lost children: whoever it may be the first essential a civilian police dog has to learn is that it only bites when told.

Guard dogs are now used by most security firms and by many property owners. Few of them are trained to anything like the police or service dog standard and some are positively dangerous, as several tragic accidents have shown. Most of them are Alsatians or Dobermans; both breeds have acquired a certain bad reputation which is undoubtedly a great deterrent to crime but which is also very unfair.

The early expeditions to the North and South Poles would have been impossible without the incredibly tough draught dogs which hauled the sledges. Even today many people living in the Arctic outback are dependent on dogs as their sole means of transport. The husky, of which there are many types and strains, is by far the commonest breed used. There are big, heavy dogs which pull weighty loads over short distances, and are also used as pack animals when there is no snow on the ground, and smaller, dogs which pull lighter loads at great speed over quite incredible distances.

Not so well known as the sledge dog of the far north were the draught dogs of Europe, now almost entirely replaced by mechanical transport. Big, strong and heavy breeds of Mastiff type, they could pull amazing loads but could never equal the efficiency of a team of huskies. At one time there were an estimated 175,000 draught dogs in Belgium where they were the main form of transport for bakers, grocers and other tradesmen. All had to hold licences and it is doubtful if any other beast of burden was surrounded by so many rules and regulations.

Draught dogs were banned from the streets of London in 1839 because of their incessant barking, and from the public highways throughout Britain in 1854 and their use is now illegal. It would appear that these dogs were pretty badly treated but it does not follow that it is cruel to put a dog in harness any more than it is to harness a horse. Either can be very cruel if the harness fits badly or if the animal strains itself with loads that are too heavy. Most dogs enjoy pulling as can be seen by anyone who watches all those dogs towing their owners along the road on a lead.

The first guide dogs were trained in Germany to help men blinded in the First World War. Mrs Dorothy Harrison Eustace, an American living in Switzerland, founded the first *Seeing Eye* organization which encouraged the setting

up of the *Master Eye Institute* in America in 1926, followed by others, including the *British Guide Dogs for the Blind Association* in 1931. Many breeds have been used for guide dogs after very careful and specialized training but the most successful breeds have proved to be Labradors and Alsatians.

Dogs have served and continue to serve man in many other ways. There are truffle hounds, rescue dogs in the Alps, film dogs and many more. Even in this age of technology we are still learning to use the dog's full potential.

Left: Labrador guide dogs at work. User and dog have to be carefully matched for compatibility and the relationship between them becomes very close. Alsatians, Golden Retrievers and Boxers are among the breeds that have been used as guides but the majority now are Labradors. Bitches are preferred because they will be less distracted by other dogs. All are spayed and quite a number of castrated dogs have proved very successful. Through her harness the guide dog can guide a blind person's steps and indicate obstructions, when to stop for traffic and when it is safe to proceed. She will guide them around all obstacles and must learn to allow for the height of her charge and ensure that there is space for them both to pass. Dog and blind person have to be carefully trained and not all blind people are suitable for using guide dogs. When they are the dog will give them enormously increased mobility and independence.

Right: College Valley Fellhounds in the north of England. See page 42.

One of the largest groups of working dogs are, of course, the Hounds. There are perhaps more packs of Foxhounds (see pg. 56) in Britain and the States than anything else, although there are many packs of Beagles and still packs of Basset hounds, Staghounds, Harriers, Otterhounds, Bloodhounds and Fellhounds, some of which are illustrated here. The Beagle was originally used for tracking hares but is now extensively used in the United States for hunting cottontail rabbits as well. Beagling is a popular sport in England in many places and the packs usually have a good following when they go out after hares. (Right) The Staffordshire Beagles setting out from the meet. They are the most adaptable of all the hounds (the domestic Basset hounds are in fact a slightly different breed to the pack hounds, which have long legs and a sturdier build) and have recently gained great popularity as pets, being a reasonable size for an indoor dog, easy to keep groomed and very well behaved. However, their popularity is eyed anxiously by their breeders and hunting people, as their excellent qualities as persistent and keen working hounds may be lost.

Top left: Staghounds setting out over the foothills of Scotland. There are not many of these packs left now, although the breeding of the hounds is carefully watched since they are bigger than Foxhounds, with longer legs and strong build in order to cover many miles and then possibly face a stag at the end of a long day's run. Fellhounds are of similar build and the packs are found on the northern moors of England. They are followed on foot.

Previous pages: The Dart Vale Harriers. The Harrier is another ancient hunting dog which was already established in Norman times. It was specifically developed to hunt the hare and is a pack animal which needs considerable discipline and is unsuitable as a domestic pet. It is larger than the Beagle, and just smaller than a Foxhound.

Left: The Culmstock Otterhounds. This pack still has several couple of the old shaggy hounds that are seldom seen today amongst the Foxhounds that make up the other packs. Their origin

is unknown but it is thought they come from Spaniel, Airedale and some Bloodhound stock as they have a very sensitive nose. Both water pollution, resulting in fewer fish and fewer otters, and the turning of public opinion against otter hunting have led to a great reduction in Otterhound numbers.

Left: The Greyhound is a very ancient breed, which used to hunt by sight. They are now the idols of the racetrack where large sums of money may be won and lost according to their performance (continued on next page).

Greyhounds are gentle and affection- ate when raised in the home but their racing prowess has eclipsed their suitability as pets. The first recorded occasion when greyhounds raced after a mechanical hare was in London in 1876. Later the sport was tried out in many places in America and was not reintroduced to Britain until 1927. Now it draws large crowds on both sides of the Atlantic. Racing Greyhounds have to be in the peak of condition and are regularly exercised by their kennel maids who walk a number of dogs at a time. Their trainer, however, will treat each dog as an individual. Training starts at about 15 months old and a healthy dog can be got running fit in about 8 weeks – probably losing 5 or 6 pounds in weight in the process. A racing Greyhound can cover a quarter of a mile in 22 seconds.

Right: A pair of Whippets. The breed was bred for coursing in northern England over a century ago and has been used for flat racing since 1894 in many countries. With the development of Greyhound racing Whippet racing declined in popularity but began a major revival in the early fifties. Today a speed of 12 seconds over a 200 yard course is not unusual.

Left: Terrier racing in Britain. These Jack Russell Terriers are not bred for racing but are ordinary working dogs which are raced as an additional excitement at some county shows.

What is a pedigree?

Wendy Boorer

MANY PEOPLE take great pride in owning a dog that has a pedigree: that is, an animal with a recorded ancestry registered with the Kennel Club. This can be a very fancy document, littered with the names of champions and other show winners, and it will certainly have a lot of long, tongue-twisting titles. The possession of this piece of paper adds quite considerably to the value of the dog.

What does it guarantee you? It means that your puppy will grow up to look very much as its parents did. It also means that your animal will be true to type and when mated with another pedigree animal of the same breed it will produce puppies of similar appearance.

Pedigrees as such are of fairly recent origin, and are closely connected with the start of dog shows and field trials. The first were held to evaluate the dog's looks and conformation, and the second to test the working abilities of gundogs. The first dog show was held in England at Newcastle upon Tyne in 1859 and the first field trial was held six years later. The early shows aroused the same kind of enthusiasm and controversy as surrounds exhibiting today and also gave rise to a number of scandals. Artful owners entered the same dog at different events under different names and it soon became apparent that, if the sport were to survive, some sort of governing body was necessary with power to make and enforce decisions in the same way as the Jockey Club did in the racing world.

In 1873 the Kennel Club was founded, followed five years later by the American Kennel Club. These institutions devise and enforce the rules and regulations under which all dog shows are run and publish stud books. These record the breeding of every dog registered with the Kennel Club and, as no unregistered dog can be shown, the stud books contain the ancestry of virtually all pedigree

Left: The Sealyham was developed as a tough and agressive Terrier by John Edwardes, of Sealyham House in Pembrokeshire, towards the end of the last century. Those dogs that did not reach his standards of courage and pugnacity were shot. The breed has retained an obstinate and self-willed streak and needs firm discipline when young. However it has shown enormous adaptability and is now better known as a domestic pet and attractive show dog. Its background gives it a strong constitution and it makes an excellent watchdog.

Right: Another even more popular Terrier is the West Highland White which usually has an engaging character and is very easy to care for. Their breeders claim that they are descended from the dogs bred at Poltalloch in Scotland since the 1800s, and although not so old a breed as the Scottish Terrier (Scottie) they do not have such a demanding breed standard. Scotties have been bred too long so that whelping is difficult.

stock. For breed enthusiasts this archetypal book of names, detailing who begat whom, can be fascinating, but it means little to the average dog owner except that the words 'KC registered' guarantee that a dog is purebred.

Many modern writers have attempted to arrange the hundreds of purebred types of dog in the world into groups distinguished by certain physical similarities – arguing that if they look alike then it is possible that their ancestry was the same. However, proof of the relationship between breeds is often difficult to establish and must often be tentative. We do know that wolves, jackals and wild dogs can be interbred with the domestic dog and produce fertile offspring. This argues that the dog has a very mixed ancestry, as is also indicated by the great diversity of dogs.

There are over 400 purebred types of dog in the world. Of them the English Kennel Club recognizes about 160, the American Kennel Club rather less. New breeds are accepted for registration but this is not an easy procedure. In England evidence is required that the breed is recognized by the Kennel Club of its country of origin, or that it has a recorded history of at least 100 years. The American Kennel Club requirements are even more stringent. Whereas in England an individual can apply to have a breed recognized so that it can be shown in variety and rare breed classes, in the States such an application must come from an active breed club with its own stud book in which some hundreds of dogs are registered across the whole country. It would no longer be possible, as has happened in the past for an individual to create a new breed by selective crossing and for it to be recognized as such. Today new breeds in the show ring are those already established elsewhere in the world, historically or numerically.

The Terrier group of 22 breeds recognized by the English and American Kennel Clubs is one that has an interesting past. Although not a great deal is known of their early history they have been bred as vermin killers for centuries and the various types have been bred true. Moreover there have been recent creations again bred for a specific working purpose, such as the Sealyham. The game little Border Terrier (left) is typical of the kind of dog bred to go to earth (the name comes from the Latin *terra*: earth) to dig out foxes, badgers and other animals. Despite its workmanlike appearance this breed is now more popular as a domestic pet than as a working dog and it adapts well, being intensely loyal and very good with children. Unlike some of its Terrier cousins its coat does not require stripping (thinning out) and its tail is never docked.

Right: Many people only think of the Yorkshire Terrier as a show dog—long coated, beribboned and seated on a cushion—but in fact they are typical Terriers and look as much when they are clipped, for the coat is rough and much like that of the other small Terriers except that it is finer and silkier. When the coat is allowed to grow the little dog looks quite different and the coat requires a great deal of attention for it does not shed and must be brushed at least once a day to remove loose hair. They are courageous, tough and lively characters and make excellent pets for those who live in small houses or flats.

Left: Two Norwich Terriers. These are very similar to the Norfolks, except that their ears are erect, whereas the Norfolks have drop ears. In the United States there is no distinction between them and one was only made in England in 1964. They are true Terriers, steady in character and make intelligent and affectionate companions.

Far top left: The Tibetan Terrier is not a Terrier at all, although its build and lively character may account for the misnomer. It was originally a small herding dog and according to legend was bred centuries ago as a mascot and watchdog in Tibetan monasteries.

Right: Dandie Dinmont (see next page).

Above: The Staffordshire Bull Terrier is probably closer to the original Bulldog and Terrier cross than the Bull Terrier itself and retains a more pugnacious appearance. It was not bred to fight bulls, that was the Bulldog's role, but was developed after bull baiting was banned in England to meet other dogs in the fighting pits. Eventually dog fighting was also prohibited but the survival of the breed is probably due to the fact that it was still carried on illegally. The breed was not recognized by the Kennel Club until the 1930s. As with the Bull Terrier, good training will produce a friendly, gentle dog, but if provoked or on guard its fighting qualities soon emerge.

Above right: The Bull Terrier is a very tough little dog, packing the maximum of muscular substance into its heavyweight frame. It is a courageous guard but can be a trifle too pugnacious towards other dogs. It is exceptionally good with children, being tough enough to enjoy the roughest game, yet always remaining sweet tempered. This is a breed which arouses great devotion amongst its fans.

Previous page: The Dandie Dinmont is a small, active, Scottish variation on the Terrier theme and is a handy size for either the town or the country. It is not quarrelsome and has a particularly loud bark, useful in a dog that is also a wonderful guard. However the melting, soulful expression under that silky topknot of hair belies an independent, not to say stubborn, character, so don't expect the ultimate in obedience.

Left: Nearly all the Terriers are popular pets, but two breeds in particular, the Scottish and the Wire Fox Terriers, had a period of extreme popularity. These bursts of favouritism are never greeted with enthusiasm by regular breeders since demand for the dogs frequently outstrips the supply of pure and well bred animals; faults creep in both in looks and temperament, and worst of all too many go as pets to unsuitable homes. Wire Fox Terriers reached the peak of their popularity in the 1930s, and their numbers have declined considerably since then. Originally they followed the hounds out hunting and would bolt the fox from its earth when necessary. They are usually strong, lively characters needing a good early training.

Below left: Here is another highly bred Terrier – the Boston Terrier is America's national breed and was probably originally developed to fight in the dog pits of the Boston area. His small size makes the Boston a popular choice for flat dwellers on both sides of the Atlantic but breeding can be difficult and most puppies have to be delivered by caesarian section. He has a great sense of fun, is determined to be one of the family and is easy to keep clean. Colour and the position of markings are considered important and in America the ears are cropped.

Left: As his looks suggest the Bedlington is the fastest and most graceful of all the Terriers and should be capable of galloping at great speed. His thick coat is very distinctive and is not given to shedding much hair, which is an advantage. They are usually devoted to their masters but can be difficult with other dogs, so it would be wise to find out in detail from an experienced breeder about the characteristics and best living conditions for these dogs; as indeed it is important to do for all breeds, but particularly in the case of those, like Terriers, that have been originally bred for specific working purposes.

Left: The Long haired Dachshund has a rich, silky coat that gives it a beauty of its own. Dachshunds originated in Germany and the long coated variety has been known there for more than 100 years. All Dachshunds are greedy dogs and unless strictly rationed will eat themselves into an early grave. Overweight dogs live short uncomfortable lives and obese Dachshunds look worse than most dogs.

Right: There are also Miniature and Standard varieties of the Wire haired Dachshund. These have not yet become as popular as the other types. They are not so exaggerated in shape and have a slightly more terrier like appearance. They are courageous and hardy with an energetic sense of fun. The harsh coat is weather resisting and the bearded chin and bushy eyebrows are very expressive.

Right: The Dachshund has the obvious appearance of having been bred for a specific purpose, which was, as its name tells, to bay badgers. It is the only hound which goes to earth like a Terrier, and its build is admirably suited for this. However intensive breeding has over emphasized the characteristic long bodies and short legs in some people's eyes, particularly in the miniatures. The standard breeds are about ten inches at the shoulder and there are three variations of coat, Smooth, Long haired and Wire haired, which also occur in the miniature types. The Miniature Smooth Dachshund is a diminutive relation of the standard form. They were created for rabbit hunting and heathy specimens will be sturdy little sporting dogs. They can be red, black and tan or chocolate in colour. Dachshunds are an adaptable breed equally suitable for town and country, but given the chance, most of them are still enthusiastic hunters of small vermin.

Right: The Pharaoh Hound is a rare breed but it is one of the most ancient types. It is a friendly and affectionate hound with a graceful appearance. Its rich red colouring and large erect ears are very striking. As its racy build suggests the breed needs a lot of exercise. It bears a striking resemblance to the hounds depicted in Egyptian temple sculptures carved 6,000 years ago.

Below: All the 'gaze' hounds are very old breeds and are probably derived from the hunting dogs of ancient Egypt. The Saluki or Gazelle Hound is one of the fastest and most elegant of dogs. There are two varieties, the feathered and the smooth, and the coat can be any colour. They are sensitive, quiet and rather withdrawn dogs except when with the people to whom they are attached. This is a breed that does need adequate exercise and which, like all the hounds, is very independent by nature.

Below: The Ibizan Hound is very like the Pharaoh Hound in build. Originating on the Spanish island of Ibiza the breed spread to the other Balearic islands where it is used to hunt rabbit, hare and partridge and trained to retrieve and point. Tourists who have seen this beautiful dog in its homeland have encouraged its popularity elsewhere. It is highly intelligent and extremely agile, being able to jump to considerable heights without a take-off run, yet it has a very gentle nature. It is a country dog and it needs plenty of exercise. The Ibizan Hound, the Pharaoh Hound and the Saluki are all the successors of the hunting dogs of the ancient Mediterranean civilizations. These dogs hunted by sight, focussing on the flicker of movement in the dry landscape and then overhauling their victims by sheer speed.

Following page: Foxhounds are probably the oldest pedigree breed, using pedigree in the sense of an animal whose ancestry has been recorded in a stud book. Some individual packs have stud books going back to the eighteenth century, whereas the Kennel Club, with whom all other breeds are registered, was not founded until 1873. The science of hound breeding was, however, known in France a great deal earlier than in most other parts of the world since it was a French saint who originated a regular breed of large black and tan hounds with good noses in the eighth century. In the seventeenth century the English settlers took their hounds to America with them and selective breeding flourished. Now, after so many centuries the foxhound is one of the most perfect animals in structure and suitability for its work.

Choosing a large breed

Wendy Boorer

How do you find out which dog will suit you best? All puppies tend to be irresistible, and since you cannot have a trial run, or trade a puppy in, as you would a car, the problem is worth a great deal of thought. Perhaps the question should first be turned the other way around. Does the way you live suit a dog? Dogs are adaptable creatures which is why they are such successful pets, but they have basic needs the fulfilment of which become the responsibility of their owners.

Dogs are sociable animals. They need companionship, so if you and your family are away at work all day choose some other pet that is less demanding in this respect. Every dog should be accustomed to being left alone quietly for three or four hours at a time, but to leave the animal alone for ten hours daily is a form of unimaginative cruelty.

Dogs need exercise, they need grooming, they need feeding—think how much time you must devote to their attention. Consider how much your dog is going to eat: feeding a large breed can be an expensive business. If having thought about these things carefully you feel that you can satisfy a dog's needs then it does not matter where you live or who you are, your dog will give you constant loyalty and affection.

Do you want to buy a pedigree dog? The initial price will be higher than that of a mongrel, but when you consider how much you will spend on its upkeep during its life the difference may seem insignificant.

There is no evidence to support the view that mongrels are either healthier or more intelligent than purebred animals. Intelligence in dogs is a very variable quality just as it is in humans. You are just as likely to end up with a moronic mongrel as a stupid thoroughbred. With a pedigree dog you will know exactly what you are getting in the way

Left: Dogs are sociable animals. They like companionship and are happy to accept you and your family as part of their pack. If everyone is working full time choose some other pet that is less demanding in this respect.

Right: The Afghan Hound is a beautiful and spectacular dog but one that makes many demands upon its owner. Being built for speed the Afghan needs miles of daily exercise and that glamorous coat must have regular daily grooming, both tasks that are a chore in wet weather. It is a dog which tends to be aloof with strangers and its independence of character makes it difficult to train.

of size and looks, and you will also have a fair idea of the kind of temperament to expect. However, the adult dog will become very much what you have made it. Your attitude to strangers and to outside events, your reactions to the puppy and to its behaviour does a lot to determine whether your dog will be a well mannered, well adjusted individual or a wild anti-social hooligan.

The question whether to buy a dog or a bitch should also be considered. This is very much a matter of personal preference and one can only generalize about the difference between the sexes. Loyalty, affection, guarding ability and obedience are qualities found in the individual dog rather than in a particular sex. Bitches are possibly more easily trained because their concentration is not being constantly distracted by the sexual signals that male animals hope to find on every tree. However, bitches come into season twice a year, a period of up to three weeks when they are sexually attractive to male dogs and have to be kept closely confined if unwanted litters are to be avoided.

Most people automatically buy a puppy when acquiring a dog, and therefore will be moulding the puppy's behaviour to suit their own particular life style. Don't however turn down an adult dog because you think it won't become attached to you; the loyalty and affection such a dog will show you depends far more upon your treatment than upon the dog's age. Always find out why an adult dog is on the market (in many cases this will be housing difficulties rather than any fault of the dog) and try to have the animal on a week's trial. This will enable you to find out whether the dog will settle in and whether it has any bad habits that you cannot tolerate. The proverb that 'you can't teach an old dog new tricks' should not be taken literally but it is very much more difficult to cure an adult dog of bad habits that it is to prevent such habits forming in a puppy.

With so many breeds registered with the Kennel Club the choice seems embarrassingly wide. Some are familiar everyday sights like the German Shepherd Dog (Alsatian), the Poodle and the Labrador. Some are so rare and exotic that they sound almost unbelievable— the hairless Chinese Crested or, at the opposite end of the scale, the Hungarian Puli, with so much hair hanging down to the ground in corded strands that it is difficult to tell at first sight whether the

dog is coming or going.

Make sure that you see your choice of breed in the flesh before committing yourself to buying. One lady decided a certain breed of Terrier looked to be just what she wanted until she heard their particularly high pitched bark, which she found so irritating that she changed her mind.

If you have made your choice of breed, where can you find your particular puppy? The best person to buy a puppy from is the person who bred it. The reasons are quite simple. Puppies are vulnerable to a number of serious and quite common infections and the less chance they have to pick these up before they reach you the better. Not only that, but each change of ownership may mean a change of diet and environment both of which are setbacks to a young animal. How difficult it is to find a dog breeder depends a great deal on how popular the breed is that you have chosen. Litters of the really well known breeds are often listed in the local newspaper. You may find that there is a show being held near you at which you can contact the local dog breeders. Alternatively there are magazines devoted to dog breeding and showing and these have extensive advertisements listing litters for sale. Finally the Kennel Club will put you in touch with the breed club serving the interests of your particular choice of dog.

Left: German Shepherds make excellent guard dogs, but a well trained dog that can be left loose is a good deal more effective than one that has to be chained. However, if premises are unenclosed so that a dog must be restrained by a chain, it is much better to use a lead attached to a ring which can slide along a wire fixed between two points. This will allow the dog greater freedom of movement which will ease its frustration and enable it to defend a much larger area.

Right: If you do not mind what breed of dog you have then why not consider adopting one of the dogs in your local dog's home? You will probably find many there with the same wistful appeal as this mongrel, which came from just such a place. Do not forget to take the dog for a medical check up as soon as possible.

Left: The Samoyed is one of the Spitz group of dogs and takes its name from a tribe of Siberian nomads who used it as a herding dog, a guard dog and to pull their sledges. It has been used by modern polar explorers, including Nansen and Captain Scott, and is noted for its endurance. Although the breed maintains some of the independence of the Arctic dogs it is happiest in human company and can easily be trained as a house dog.

Left: The Chow is a dog of leonine appearance with a stilted gait and a blue black tongue that are unique in the canine world. He tends to be aloof and detached with strangers but entirely devoted to his owner. As a guard dog the Chow is not to be trifled with. The profuse coat tends to create problems and Chows can suffer considerable distress in heatwaves.

Right: The aristocratic bearing of the Borzoi is a reminder that this was the dog of the princes and boyars of Imperial Russia. Bred from a Saluki-like dog of the Middle East, crossed with northern shepherd dogs to give the warmer coat needed in the Russian winter, this beautiful and intelligent dog was used for coursing the wolf. A perfectly matched pair of these fast hounds would be slipped when a wolf had been beaten out of cover. Their task was to pursue the wolf and, striking together, bring him down for the huntsman to ride up and dispatch with his dagger. Aloof in manner and somewhat suspicious of strangers, the Borzoi can nevertheless be very affectionate to those whom it accepts. It is not recommended where there are young children for it does not happily accept any affront to its dignity Although it is no longer used to pursue wolves it still requires plenty of space, leisure to complete its grooming and a princely income to satisfy its appetite.

Left: Dogs the size of a Great Dane need firm early training if they are to become well mannered adults. The bed this dog is lying on is ideal, being raised from the floor to protect the animal from draughts. The mattress, with its washable cover, is essential for the heavy-weight, giant breeds who tend to develop callouses if they have to lie on hard surfaces.

Above: Puppies often look very similar... this is a Bull Mastiff, and, as its name suggests, is a cross between the Bulldog and the Mastiff. It was developed towards the end of the last century to aid gamekeepers in catching poachers. They needed a dog which was faster and more aggressive than the Mastiff and larger than the Bulldog, and they trained it to keep quiet and to attack only on command. A dark brindled colouring was originally preferred, since this made it difficult to see in the dark, but today's dogs are fawn or red with a dark muzzle.

Left: The American Cocker Spaniel, officially known in the United States simply as the Cocker Spaniel, has its origin in the same stock as the English type but it also carries a gene for a long and profuse coat. It is still used as a gundog but is most popular as a pet. It makes a merry and active companion but owners must be prepared for the work that caring for its coat entails.

Above: The Basenji is classed as a hound, being a hunting dog from the Congo basin. It is a streamlined dog with upstanding ears, and a heavily wrinkled forehead, and a tail tightly curled over the back. It is more usually red in colour and, like all hounds, has a stubborn streak. The breed is peculiar in that it does not bark, but it more than makes up for this by a series of rather unmelodious howls.

Left: Ownership of the aristocratic Scottish Deerhound was once restricted to persons of the rank of Earl or higher and it was the companion of Highland Chieftans, but its numbers dwindled when the clan system collapsed. The enthusiasm of Queen Victoria and eminent Victorians such as the painter Landseer and the novelist Walter Scott revived its popularity, but it is a big dog requiring more space and exercise than most people are prepared to provide today.

Top right: The Basset Hound is still very much a hunting dog. It is a large dog on short legs and needs a great deal of exercise, which must be supervised, as even in domestic pets the hunting instinct is still quite strong. It is not an ideal town dog for, despite that soulful exterior, it is a strong, active animal with the stubborn streak common to many hounds.

Left: Poodles are one of the most popular dogs in the world. They come in three sizes: Standard, Miniature and Toy. The largest or Standard Poodle is shown here and was probably the original of this intelligent family. The Poodle was first used by wildfowlers for retrieving game from water, but being easily taught and a dog with a sense of fun, it has played many roles since then, from fashion accessory to circus acrobat. Its coat is clipped in a variety of styles of which the 'Lion' clip is one of the most traditional. Poodles can be any solid colour, though they are usually black, white or dark brown. This Standard Poodle has his brown coat clipped short but without any fancy trim giving a much more natural look than the more elaborate styles. It is also easier to see its relationship with the Water Spaniels much more clearly.

Choosing a smaller breed

Wendy Boorer

Above: The Cavalier King Charles Spaniel is a type of dog that has been known since Elizabethan times at least. The old names of 'Comforter' and 'Spanielle gentle' aptly describe its function in life. In fact the modern breed, sometimes known as the Blenheim Spaniel, is a recreation of the older type from the King Charles Spaniel, which had developed into a smaller dog. However, like all Spaniels of whatever size it has a sporting side and enthusiasts have used it as a gundog. This pair live in California.

Centre: The Shetland Sheepdog had its origin as a working dog but it is now a very popular pet. Like Shetland ponies, the 'Sheltie' is not an artificially produced miniature but owes its small size

to a natural adaption of the Collie type to its island home. Its dainty appearance has led to the nickname 'faerie' dog. The breed has all the Collie virtues but timid specimens should be avoided.

Right: The Lhasa Apso is a small guard dog of Tibetan origin. The long coat obviously needs time spent to keep it in order but this is a dog of great charm and personality. The breed comes in a variety of attractive colours and particolours, but golden and honey are preferred. It is usually excellent with children, is longlived and makes a good house dog.

Far right: Europe's oldest lapdog, the Maltese, and a puppy from one of the more recent breeds to become known

in the West, the Shih Tzu, which was not recognized by the American Kennel Club until 1969. The Maltese has been known since Roman times at least. Its good nature and high spirits make it a popular pet but its coat demands a great deal of attention. The Shih Tzu (the name means Lion Dog in Chinese) appears frequently in Chinese art but it is actually a breed from Tibet. It is said that it was the custom for Chinese visitors to Tibet to be given these Lion Dogs which thus became established in China. Like the Maltese it needs daily brushing and careful combing. As the top knot grows it falls into the eyes so should be tied up to keep the dog's vision clear. If you are not thinking of showing your dog you could trim it off instead.

Top: This puppy and its mother belong to the rough-coated variety of the Griffin Bruxellois. There is also a smooth coated form which is more properly known as the Petit Brabançon. A cheeky-faced, intelligent breed, it was originally a stable dog whose job was to keep down the rats and it has much of the character of a Terrier. Although hardy when adult this is a difficult dog to breed and rear, which may account for the fact that it is not very well known.

Above: Among the rarest and most bizarre of all the breeds is the Chinese Crested Dog. The hairless skin is fine and silky to the touch and attractively mottled with various colours. The head carries a crest of flowing hair, there is hair on the feet and a plume on the end of the tail. They are affectionate and active little dogs who need to be protected from cold and from sunburn. Like all rarities the hairless breeds are difficult to find and expensive to buy.

Left: In contrast to the Borzoi the Italian Greyhound is the smallest of the greyhound group. It is claimed that it is a very ancient breed and it appears in many renaissance paintings. It is a lively dog and a keen hunter which requires plenty of exercise but because of its small size can keep fit with access to even a smallish garden. It is a particularly clean dog with a smooth coat that requires no more grooming than a rub down with a duster and it has no 'doggy' odour, making it an excellent house companion.

Right: The Jack Russell Terrier does not have the benefit of a pedigree or Kennel Club blessing but it is a very popular dog. Today's Jack Russells do not look particularly like the dogs kept by the Devonshire parson whose name they carry because he did not attempt to breed a type but rather chose good working dogs, mainly types of Wire haired Fox Terrier, but they are an easily recognizable type of short-legged Terrier. Still actively used as a working dog, the Jack Russell is as hard as nails and full of pep and vigour. No proper Jack Russell can resist investigating a hole!

Left: The Toy Poodle has all the charm of a very small dog combined with the fun-loving acrobatic ability of its larger relations. However like all Poodles, Toys carry a very heavy harsh-textured coat. Not only must this be clipped at intervals, it must also be brushed and combed daily to prevent it felting into impenetrable mats.

Right: The Papillon or Butterfly Dog
gets its name from its upstanding
fringed ears which resemble the wings
of a butterfly. Ideally there should be a
narrow, white, clearly defined blaze up
the forehead which is supposed to
represent the butterfly body. This tiny
toy breed is a bundle of acrobatic
energy. Not only is it very active, it is
also very intelligent. Papillons have
been used in obedience work and
delight in learning tricks. The
youngster in the picture has yet to
develop the fringes on the ears and legs
that are part of the attraction of the
adult coat.

Preceeding page: Because puppies are
so appealing, you should consider
carefully what you want in your dog
before falling for one in a pet shop and
think hard before going out to buy one.
This trio are Golden Cocker Spaniels.
Despite their soulful look they are
happy, active dogs with a sense of
humour, who delight in human
companionship but who also need
regular grooming and a certain amount
of trimming. Like all breeds with hairy
legs and feet they will bring in wet and
mud in plenty.

Above: The Bulldog is a strikingly massive breed for his height but, despite his appearance and his bull-baiting background, is usually a placid, dignified and affectionate dog. The exaggerated shape of the skull has made many specimens susceptible to breathing difficulties and ultimately to heart trouble, so this is not a suitable dog for the energetic walker.

Right: The Japanese Spaniel, or Chin Chin, may share a common ancestry with the Pekinese and the Pug. It was the pet of the Japanese court and nobility and the first dogs to travel to the West were taken from Japan by Commodore Perry in 1835. In the middle of the last century an English writer declared that its small size had been obtained by rearing the dogs on *sake*! It makes a lively companion but needs careful grooming.

Left: Reactions to the personable Pug often run to extremes. People either think it ugly or quite enchanting. It is said to be an ancient Chinese breed, perhaps the smooth-coated version of the Pekinese, and references to similar dogs occur in Chinese literature of more than 2,500 years ago. It is a solidly built dog but its compact body, short head and apparent lack of neck make it seem much smaller than it is. The very short neck and face conformation make the Pug breathe noisily–whether you call it a snuffle or a snore depends on how you regard the breed. It is a tough, intelligent dog and very tolerant.

Left: The Tibetan Spaniel is another of the four Tibetan breeds known in Britain. Like all the Tibetan breeds, the Tibetan Spaniel is a cheeky and independent character with a great sense of his own importance. The coat is soft, silky and flat; the most popular colours are cream, golden and fawn.

Below: The Pekinese is Britain's most popular toy dog breed. If it is not spoilt by doting owners, the Pekinese is a sporting little dog full of guts and character. The long, profuse adult coat can be any colour and needs regular and careful grooming. Although it is a tough little dog it's protruding eyes are unfortunately liable to injury.

Right: The Pomeranian is a dwarf version of the Spitz type dog. It is an active and vivacious breed but has a bad reputation for yapping.

Training a dog

John Holmes

AN OBEDIENT DOG is usually much happier than a disobedient one. The owner and everyone else the dog comes into contact with will also be much happier if he comes when he is called, follows to heel and stays where he is told. In order to teach a dog these things you must forget any ideas you may have about dogs being almost human. Fortunately for us they are not.

The dog is one of the easiest animals to train, not because of his superior intelligence – the cat, for instance, is just as intelligent – but because it is a pack animal with a strong instinct to follow a leader, while the cat simply goes its own way and is virtually untrainable. The dog is willing, sometimes anxious, to accept a human master as a leader, while

the cat will only accept him as a friend.

There is a snag. Dogs vary enormously in their degree of dominance and submissiveness, from the born leader to the lowest member of the pack; and the same applies to human beings. If a dominant dog falls into the hands of a submissive owner it may well prove quite untrainable although it could be an excellent dog with a dominant owner. Because I believe this to be the prime cause of many dog/owner problems I have become more convinced that the first essential to successful training is finding the right dog to train.

Dogs do not reason as we do. They learn by association of ideas. We learn in exactly the same way, especially when we are young. A five-year old child will

understand you when you warn him 'If you put your finger near the fire you will get burnt', but a year-old baby will not and has to be prevented from going near the fire by a fireguard. If, accidentally, he gets burnt he is unlikely to need warning about fires again. He will associate the painful experience with the fire and avoid it for a very long time.

Naturally, a dog tends to repeat the actions which it finds pleasant and to refrain from doing the things it finds unpleasant so in training we try to make it pleasant for the dog to do the things we want it to do and unpleasant for it to do the things we don't want it to do. We must be careful not to build up the wrong associations accidentally. It is a strange fact that if a child gets bitten

Right: If a pup pesters his mother she will growl at him. Most pups respond to this sound and resist from pulling mum's tail or ear or whatever else they are doing to annoy her. Sometimes a dominant pup will continue to pester, whereupon the bitch snaps at it, often quite severely, and it immediately stops. Usually the bitch will then lick and caress the pup, as this Shih Tzu is doing, and it will stop crying. But next time it hears a growl it will associate the sound with a nasty snap and stop whatever it is doing. If dog owners would adhere to this simple and uncomplicated policy there would be fewer badly behaved dogs.

Far right: This well-mannered little Cairn Terrier is making his request in the politest possible way. Most dogs learn to beg without any difficulty. Some will beg almost instinctively and others will pick up the idea if you hold a titbit just out of their reach, but not so high that they feel encouraged to jump for it.

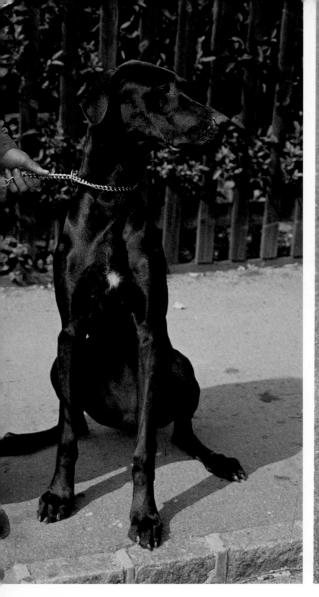

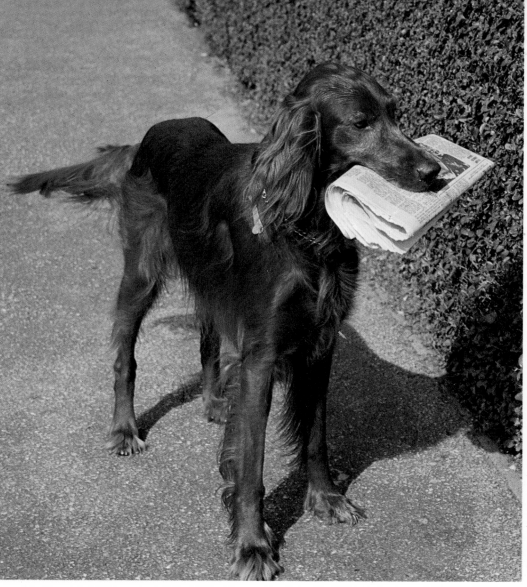

by a dog he is excused of being afraid of dogs for the rest of his life, but if a dog is kicked by a child it is considered stupid if it is afraid of children and nasty if aggressive towards them.

You should start all training in a place familiar to the dog and away from distractions. To teach him to come when called see that he is somewhere from which it is impossible for him to escape. If he will not come to you in the house or garden the chances of his coming to you in the park are nil. With a new dog or puppy that knows nothing, wait until he shows signs of coming to you, crouch down, extend a hand with fingers moving (forget anything you may have heard about shoving the back of your hand towards a dog) and call him by his name followed by 'come', 'here' or whatever word you intend using thereafter.

Dogs respond instinctively to varying tones of voice and this is a great help in training. It is not what you say but how you say it that is important so use the nicest, friendliest tone of voice that you can manage. Almost certainly the pup will come to you. Then you can offer him a tit-bit and make a great fuss of him.

Next time he hears the same sound (his name followed by 'here') in the same tone of voice he will associate it with reward and should come to you. But he will not associate it with anything if the whole family keep repeating his name and calling him from all directions at the same time. All that will teach him is to ignore his name completely, just as he ignores a sound which is constantly repeated on the radio.

Many dogs learn *not* to come when called by owners who believe they are punishing them for running away. You should wait until the dog has returned and then praise it for coming back; it is too late to punish it for running away. A young or untrained dog associates correction or reward with what it is doing or is about to do, not with what it has done. What is on its mind is what matters, not what its body is doing. That is why a bright young dog, punished when he returns to his owner, quickly learns that when he hears his master's voice calling in an angry tone the safest thing to do is to keep well out of reach. Therefore remember always to praise him well when he comes back, no matter what he has done.

In my opinion the most useful of all obedience exercises is the 'Down'. An obedient dog should stay where it is told and the easiest way to teach it that is by training the dog to lie down – and stay there. A dog lying down cannot bite someone walking past a few yards away, nor jump up and leave muddy marks on the best suit of a non-doggy guest. Even if he won't come to you, provided he stays there, you can go to him and attach a lead. Perhaps most important of all is that teaching a dog to lie down quietly beside you for long periods will do its temperament a lot of good. Indeed it is the only way I know of steadying down an over excitable dog which continually fusses and fumes around the place.

You cannot over-reward a dog when he does right and you should never forget to give him praise. Nor should you fail to correct him when he does wrong, but match the rebuke not so much to the 'crime' committed as to the dog that you are training. By following these principles you should be able to teach your dog much more than the exercises given here. You will find that the more you teach him—the more you are the leader—the more attached to you he will become.

Far left: Always encourage your dog to sit whenever he reaches the edge of a kerb then, should he go out into the street at any time without a lead he will not rush across the road without your order. Even if you always make sure he is on a lead when in traffic areas, which you should certainly do, this will avoid any risk of him attempting to cross the road and causing an accident.

Left: Most dogs enjoy performing a few tricks or chores, such as carrying your paper. It is a game for them and they like to please you. Sometimes they will do something spontaneously which, if you praise them, they will enjoy repeating.

Left: If your dog has already learned to ignore his name you will have to resort to correction. One way of doing this is with a check cord. Provided that the dog is familiar with a collar and lead you can take him to a park or open space with about 30 feet of cord attached to his collar. Allow him to run 'free' and call his name in a friendly tone. If he does not respond change the tone of the voice completely – the *tone* not the volume – and repeat the command as a command, not a request. If he responds to this, reward him lavishly. If he does not, you must follow the command with a sharp jerk on the cord. If he now responds go back to the friendly tone immediately and coax him right up to you. The lead or check cord serves two purposes. It enables you to provide correction when the dog is close to you and it prevents the dog running away. When it is removed you cannot correct the dog but you can still reward him, so the object is to get him to respond for reward rather than because of the correction.

Left: To teach a dog to lie down first hold the long lead used in training in the right hand and allow it to hang in a loop from the hand back up to the dog's collar. Now put the left foot on the loop, as the owner of the Cavalier King Charles Spaniel is doing, at the same time placing the left hand on the shoulder, and pull the lead through your instep with the right hand.

Left: Another method is first to teach the dog to sit by pulling back with the collar in the right hand and at the same time pushing the dog's rump down with the left. Now place the right hand behind his knees and the left top of his shoulders. Say 'Down', and pull his front legs forward from below him at the same time push him down with the left hand on his shoulders, as the owner is doing to this Bloodhound pup. When he is down, probably after a struggle, praise him gently by tone of voice and by stroking his head. (Dogs hate being patted on the head, although many are forced to endure it.) If you praise him too enthusiastically the chances are that he will get up. As soon as he stops struggling and relaxes for a fraction of a second let him get up and start again. If you do not he may start struggling once more and you will end up in a battle which he may well win. Each time you repeat the exercise he should go down more easily and stay quiet longer. From here it is just a question of time before he associates the sound 'Down' with the action and lies down without having to be pushed.

Above: This German Shepherd Dog knows that a raised hand means 'Sit'.

Left: Bad habits are easy to nip in the bud but often impossible to cure once they have become established. Pulling on the lead is one of them, as with this Bernese Mountain dog and Lurcher. The mistake so often made is to pull against the dog, which soon begins to enjoy pulling. Provided that the dog pulls through enjoyment and not because he is afraid he should be *jerked* back into position by the lead. When he is in position praise him well. Soon he should associate pulling with a sharp jerk and walking on a slack lead with a reward.

Looking after your dog

Alan Hitchins

Dogs are carnivorous. You need look no further than a dog's teeth to see that it is a meat eater, for its dentition is suited to the tearing and chewing of flesh. Its digestive system has no modifications to cope with herbivorous material. In the wild the dog is a hunter and scavenger and survived for centuries on a diet of meat and bone, although in times of hunger wild dogs do eat grubs, berries and some greenstuff. Therefore domesticated dogs should be fed a diet principally of meat and any substitutes should be of high protein content.

From within 24 hours of birth to approximately 6 weeks old the young pup suckles milk from its mother, although from 4 weeks most puppies can successfully be given milk or milk substitutes, with some solid food to lap up. Commercial baby foods are useful here, or milk mixed with finely chopped meat such as chicken or fish. At six weeks the pup should be feeding itself on four meals daily. A normal programme would be a morning feed of cereals and milk, shredded or well chopped meat (cooked or raw) at midday and early evening, followed by a late evening meal of milk.

At about four months of age this can be reduced to three meals a day, then at six months to two. By one year old one meal a day should be sufficient, the quantities being increased as the puppy grows.

An adult dog's requirements vary considerably according to its size and

All dogs need plenty of exercise. Fortunately most of them enjoy retrieving, like this German Shepherd Dog who is seen jumping over a stream in pursuit.

Left: The ecstacy of a roll after being indoors.

Above: All puppies need toys but there is no need to buy special ones: a worn out slipper, an empty cardboard carton, a cotton reel and a piece of string are what this Norwich Terrier chose for himself.

Right: Like this puppy, all dogs enjoy burying their treasure but do not let them dig around garbage and rubbish dumps in case they inadvertantly injure themselves on sharp metal or broken glass.

build. A certain amount of food is needed to maintain normal metabolic processes and extra food is required for activity beyond this. Quantity must be related to the dog's way of life. For example, a working sheepdog requires much more food than a dog of equal size living in town. A large dog such as an Alsatian requires about two pounds of meat a day whereas for a small dog like a Fox Terrier about six to eight ounces will suffice. The best way to judge an individual dog's needs is to observe its weight. If it is fat, reduce the intake; if thin, increase it. Appetite is a poor guide since dogs in the wild will immediately eat whatever they can obtain, in case they lack food the next day. By instinct the modern dog still tends to eat all that is put in front of him. The result is the only too common overweight problem seen in household dogs. The diet should include protein in the form of lean fresh meat, carbohydrates such as bread or cereal and fat, which may be dripping, lard, margarine, butter or any vegetable oil. There should be twice as much protein as carbohydrates and about one tenth of the total weight should be fat, remembering that even lean meat contains a little fat.

Loss of condition, a staring coat, loss of weight, dull eyes, lethargy and even too much weight may indicate an incomplete diet or a lack of balance on which you should seek veterinary advice.

Naturally there are times when a special diet is necessary. If your dog has been ill your veterinarian will probably recommend a special high protein diet, and conditions such as nephritis and diabetes will make their own demands, but the most frequent alteration to diet is for the pregnant bitch. For the first three weeks of her eight to nine week gestation period there need be little more food than usual but in the following two weeks there should be an increase of fifty per cent. By the last week of gestation food intake should be back to normal. Extra protein and plenty of milk or a calcium supplement will ensure well formed pups and prevent calcium deficiency in the bitch. Supplements of vitamins A and D will reduce the risk of congenitally deformed puppies.

To prevent accidents when you go out with your dog you will obviously keep him on a leash until you are in a park or open country well away from traffic, but even in our parks and in ponds and streams careless people often leave dan-

gerous litter and it is easy for a dog to get a cut or scratch. This will probably not not cause serious bleeding but even small cuts need washing and bandaging to keep dirt out so that they will not become infected. Small cuts on the ear, however, rarely stop bleeding by themselves and require careful treatment to avoid excessive loss of blood.

On the limbs deeper cuts with severe bleeding should be controlled by making a tourniquet—in an emergency a tie and a piece of soft cloth such as a handkerchief could be used—but no tourniquet should be left on longer than 20 minutes at a time. Get veterinary attention as soon as possible so that the wound can be properly cleaned out and dressed and antibiotic treatment given. Stitching might also be necessary in some cases.

If you suspect a dog to have a fractured bone in the leg it should be supported by a splint to prevent further damage as you take it to the vet, but for any other injury wrap the dog up in a blanket.

In almost all severe accidents there is some degree of shock for the animal. The first symptoms are a paleness of the gums and an inability to move. Although there may be no sign of external injury the dog needs immediate veterinary attention,

Above: Active dogs burn up a lot of
energy in a day and need a good supply
of carbohydrates. Proprietary dog
biscuits will supply all the carbohydrates that a dog needs and about a
third to half the protein depending on
the kind of biscuit used. If you feed a
so called 'complete diet' you should
supplement it with milk and some
fresh meat. Unless the diet consists of
high quality meat you should add
supplements of vitamins A and B,
calcium and phosphate. Raw meat is
most nutritious and you should vary
between, for example, beef, chicken,
rabbit and horse. Cooking destroys
some of the vitamins and other con-
stituents but reduces the possibility of
infection. Offal has poor nutritional
value and variation in quality makes
it difficult to balance the diet. Canned
meats are sterile and safe and are
usually lean, but quality can vary
considerably.

Left: A vet re-dresses a wound after a
successful treatment while the Chow
Chow's owner reassures her dog.

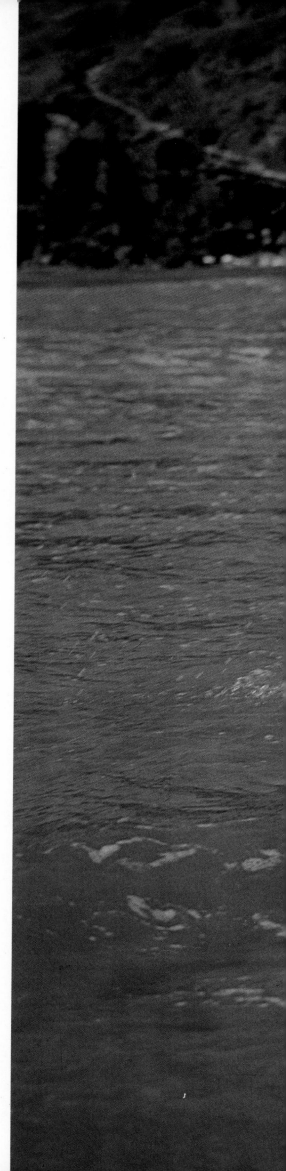

Left: A bitch's milk has to supply carbohydrates, protein, fat and calcium and phosphate for her growing pups. She is able to supply these from her own tissue but it is better to make sure that she is given an adequate diet so that it will not be necessary. Increased amounts of food, supplemented by bone meal, milk and a multivitamin source should be given, the quantities being reduced as the pups begin to be weaned. Plenty of water is essential for her to produce sufficient milk.

for shock reaction can lead to death in only a few hours. Any form of eye injury should also be treated immediately even if bleeding does not occur. Wasp and bee stings are usually only serious when they occur in the mouth and the consequent swelling obstructs breathing.

Naturally, you will take care that all poisons are kept where the dog cannot get at them, but it is not possible to protect a dog from poisons laid by others. Vomiting is often the main symptom, followed by collapse in a few hours. Common rat poisons often produce bleeding of the gums and vomiting of blood. If you know a dog has eaten a poisonous substance force it to swallow a crystal of washing soda or a strong salt solution. If this is given within three hours of eating the poison there will be a reasonable chance that the dog will vomit it back before it has been absorbed.

Vomiting may also be caused by an object lodged in the intestine: chicken and chop bones are particularly dangerous in this way and surgery is often necessary to remove them. Always treat vomiting as worth a vet's attention.

Never lock a dog in a closed car or any other confined space without making sure that there is adequate ventilation. On a hot day the body temperature may rise rapidly, causing the dog to collapse from heat stroke. The simplest effective treatment is to soak the dog in cold water until it recovers.

The most common diseases to which dogs are subject are caused by parasites. Fleas are a frequent irritant. The small, red-brown, hard-coated dog flea moves extremely quickly, is hard to catch and difficult to see when on the dog. Small black specks on the skin and sores from scratching are signs of its presence. Occasionally dogs develop an allergy to fleas and break out in lumps and sores over the body, although only one or two fleas may be present. The most effective way of

eliminating fleas is to use a fleabath regularly or to follow a control routine available from your vet.

Other external parasites are lice and ticks. Lice are seen as white specks in the hair, usually in clusters and moving slowly. Closer examination shows they have a light orange colour. They are very irritating, causing distress and violent scratching, but can be killed by common parasiticidal baths. In summer ticks may be picked up from long grass. They look like small black peas attached to the skin. Do not pull them out but apply methylated spirit to kill them, then they can be picked off with ease. If they cause abscesses call the vet.

Mange is a skin condition produced by various mites which infest the skin causing irritation. They spread slowly over the dog causing a very severe condition that may result in death. Mange is contagious to humans so at the first sign of a diffuse, scaly skin condition coupled with hair loss you should see the vet.

Ear mites are similar to the mange mite and may first be indicated by the dog constantly scratching his ears, and confirmed by an inflamed-looking ear with a dark brown wax inside it. Untreated it can result in deformed ears and possibly in loss of balance.

Small abrasions in the ear caused by scratching or by a foreign object, such as a grass seed, may produce bacterial infection, characterized by puss and a strong smell, which should be treated rapidly. Prolonged ear scratching can make the layers of the ear become separated and fill with blood. This condition, called Aural haematoma, looks like a swollen ear. An operation is usually necessary for cure.

'Ringworm' is not a worm but a fungus infection which is first noticed as small bald patches, often in the shape of a ring (hence the common name). Such fungal conditions spread easily from one

Left: A pair of Dalmatians enjoying themselves at the seaside.

---

dog to another and may affect people, leaving scars on the skin. The dog should be treated as soon as the infection is discovered and your own doctor consulted regarding possible human infection.

Roundworms and tapeworms are internal parasites. Roundworms are especially common in puppies who often contract worms from their mother before birth. They vomit them up or pass them in their stools. These worms are quite long, pale yellow to white in colour, round and often curled at the ends. The affected puppy usually has a swollen, tense stomach, cries for no apparent reasons, moves uncomfortably, develops diarrhoea and loses weight.

Tapeworms can be distinguished from roundworms by their flat appearance and they are divided into segments. Often the first sign is broken off segments in the stools. They are small, mobile and resemble grains of rice. Tapeworms cause diarrhoea, loss of weight and often produce vomiting with some blood. Both kinds of worms can be treated by appropriate pills, but get them from your vet to make sure that the pill and the dose are correct. Both parasites can be passed to humans, especially children.

Two of the most serious diseases dogs can catch are distemper and viral hepatitis. Distemper is unfortunately common and usually fatal. It is often seen in young puppies, although all ages are susceptible. The first signs are a cough, vomiting, loss of appetite, diarrhoea and a yellow discharge from the eyes and the nose. As the disease progresses twitches and fits develop. Although the disease lasts for weeks, immediate attention is necessary for any hope of recovery.

Viral hepatitis is a disease affecting the liver and can also be fatal if left untreated. It is not a very common condition. Often the only signs are weakness, lethargy and weight loss. The dog has a very high temperature and usually pants. Jaundice eventually develops.

Fortunately the most serious common diseases, including distemper, viral and a bacterial hepatitis and a bacterial kidney infection, can be prevented by vaccination. Normally two vaccinations are given, one at ten and the other at twelve weeks of age, although an earlier vaccination is possible.

Showing off

Wendy Boorer

Dog shows are beauty competitions where the construction, shape and movement of one animal is compared with another, and both are measured against the breed standard, a portrait in words of what the ideal dog of that breed should look like. Every breed that is shown has its own standard, a description that was originally written or approved by the parent club which looked after that particular breed's interests. This description was then approved by and lodged with the Kennel Club, who reserve the right to restrict its reproduction. Breed standards vary in their quality according to the ability of the people who wrote them. A written description is open to a number of interpretations. These two factors give dog showing the fascination of unpredictability because if everyone agreed as to which was the best dog, showing would stop. As it is, the really great dogs in each breed are generally recognized by judges and win pretty consistently. Good quality animals, who are not quite top-flight, will have a more chequered career, winning one day under a judge who likes their type and being ignored another day by a judge who is impressed by something rather different. Really poor breed specimens won't win anywhere and eventually they are withdrawn from showing.

What do dog shows accomplish? They have now been in existence for well over 100 years during which time they have steadily increased in popularity. Looking back over that span of time one can see that the appearance of many breeds has been greatly improved and that all breeds are much more standardized and uniform. Public interest in pedigree livestock has grown tremendously and the show ring provides the publicity that each breed requires if it is to survive. This factor is very important, as every dog breeder depends on the sale of surplus puppies to the public as pets. Nearly

Left: This ring full of Basset Hounds, being shown in the summer sun, seems a far cry from the breed's original function of hunting the hare. The exhibitors are all on their knees positioning their low-to-ground hounds to the best advantage. The dogs themselves take very little notice of each other, having been taught that sniffing or attempting to play with their neighbour is not acceptable behaviour.

Right: Toy dogs, like this long-coated Chihuahua are benched in small wire cages, rows of which are placed on trestle tables. These cages are often lined with curtains and cushions by owners anxious to show off their animals to the best advantage. The dog's number, which identifies it in the catalogue and show ring, can be seen on the front of the cage.

Above: The ideal showdog will stand posed to the best advantage at the end of a loose lead. As will be seen from this picture of a Saluki, this is by far the most effective and eye-catching way of exhibiting an animal. However it requires a great deal of training which must start long before the animal is entered for its first show. The show puppy should have daily lessons in standing and posing and it must also be taught to accept the sort of examination which the judge will give. The judge will examine its mouth and run his hands over the dog's body to assess its construction. Self control on the part of the exhibitor is important too. Many owners tend to fidget round their animals in the show ring, distracting both the dog and judge!

Right: The Bearded Collie is one of the breeds which has a double coat. The long harsh, straight outer coat sheds water easily and keeps the dog dry. The soft, woolly undercoat keeps the dog warm whatever conditions it was called upon to face in its original capacity as a sheepdog. As too much combing tends to remove the undercoat, most of the grooming on this breed will be done with a brush. The coat will be tackled in layers so that the brush can get right down to the roots of the hair. The dog here has been trained to sit on a table to make his owner's job easier.

Left: This famous Akita Champion, photographed in an appropriately oriental setting, obtained his title by a different system. In Australia and the United States the coveted title of Champion is awarded on points, the number of points a dog gains being geared to the type of show, the nature of the dog's wins and the number of the opposition.

Right: Adult Poodles are always shown in the lion clip. Opinions vary as to the origin of this fashion. One theory is that the hindquarters were shaved so that the hair did not impede the dog when it was swimming, for the Poodle was originally a gundog used for retrieving waterfowl. The pompoms of hair left on the legs were to protect the joints from cold. Another theory is that the lion clip is based on the court dress of Louis XIV, and represents the full bottomed wig and ruffles of the period. Small dogs like this Miniature Poodle are placed on a table to be examined by the judge.

every breed was originally created to do a specific job of work. As mechanization and urbanization removed the need for dogs to take cattle to market, or turn spits, or pull carts, the kinds of dogs that did these jobs tended to die out. The number of extinct breeds is quite a long one, but many others were saved from disappearing by the interest of show exhibitors. A rare breed must be campaigned in the show ring to gain the publicity necessary for its survival.

What the show ring cannot do is measure a dog's working ability. The winner of a beauty contest may take your eye but you cannot tell what she would be like to live with, and the same thing applies with a winning dog. One can assume that the temperament of a winner is sound. After all it has just been examined intimately by the judge, who is probably a total stranger, and it has shown neither fear nor aggression. As it has won, one can assume that the dog is constructed soundly enough to do its original job of work. What one cannot assume is that the dog has the ability, the drive or the brains for its original job. How much this matters depends on your point of view. Those who want working gundogs or working sheepdogs buy them from working stock rather than show stock. Many working dogs aren't suitable as pets having tremendous energy and a compulsion to work which need to be utilised if the animal is not to become neurotic and destructive. Most pet owners want a placid friendly animal and this temperament is equally necessary in a show dog.

A more serious criticism of the show ring is that in some breeds physical peculiarities have been exaggerated until they have become a hazard to the dog's health. The reasons for this can very often be found in a poorly worded breed standard. A description written 70 years ago saying that the nose should be as short as possible has led to a modern dog with breathing difficulties and a tendency to skin troubles in the deeply folded wrinkles on its face. Some body shapes predispose an animal to whelping difficulties, or spinal trouble. These are some of the rather more insidious dangers that occur when dogs are bred solely for their looks.

The ruling body in the dog show world is the Kennel Club with whom every dog must be registered before it can be shown. The Kennel Club licences all shows and enforce the rules and regulations under which all shows are run. There are basically four types of show ranging from the small local event held in an evening, with some 70 or so competitors, to the big annual Champion-

Right: Tradition decrees that Yorkshire Terriers are shown posed on top of their gaily decorated travelling boxes. Many hours will be spent keeping the coat of a breed like this in top condition. As length of coat is important with a Yorkshire Terrier, these dogs will have their hair oiled and rolled up in paper curlers between shows. This treatment prevents the hair becoming brittle and breaking. Though to the layman a Yorkshire Terrier in curlers may look rather ridiculous, it should be remembered that these tiny dogs thoroughly enjoy the fuss and attention they get while being groomed.

Left: Winning means very little in terms of money but a great deal in terms of prestige. This West Highland White, surrounded by trophies and rosettes, is photographed so that his owner can record the thrill of an achievement that by the nature of things can only be short lived. In Britain a dog has to win three Challenge Certificates under three different judges. The number of Challenge certificates on offer each year for a particular breed is proportional to the number of animals registered in the preceding year.

ship shows which are spread over 2 or 3 days and may cater for 7,000 dogs. Each country where dog shows are held classifies its shows differently and grades the breed classes using different criteria, but in all the most coveted title to be gained by a show dog is that of Champion.

Obviously every exhibitor wants to breed and show a top flight dog, but even a top flight dog will not be the winner unless trained and presented to perfection. The bloom and sparkle of perfect health are necessities for success and are achieved by a first class diet and carefully controlled exercise. Good movement in the show ring and grooming play their part and some training for the show ring will help your dog to show itself to its best advantage.

Right: At all the major shows the dogs are benched when they are not actually in the show ring. This enables spectators to view the dogs all the time. This Irish Wolfhound looks as if he has had a long day!

Index

Acknowledgments

The publishers would like to thank the following organizations and individuals for their kind permission to reproduce the pictures in this book: AFA Colour Library 76 top. Alpha 27. Australian News and Information Bureau 15. Victor Baldwin 13, 23 bottom, 55, 68 left, 92. Barnaby's Colour Library 17. Bavaria Verlag 7 (M Mackus), 62 bottom (H Bielfeld), 87 bottom (J Zeitbild), 88 (H Heimpel). Camera Press 4–5, 18, 29 top, 52 top, 68 centre, 96, Bruce Coleman 85, Colour Library International 10 top right, 24–5, 88–9. Commissioner of Police 34, 36, 37 top. Ann Cumbers 1, 6, 8, 20, 33 top, 47, 48 top right, 50 top left, 51 top, 54, 64, 65 top, 66 centre, 69, 70 centre left, 75, 91, 92 bottom, 93. F P G Inc 32. J Good, NHPA 12 bottom, 30 bottom, 31. Greyhound Racing Association 43 bottom, 44 top. Sonia Halliday Photographs 76 bottom. J Meads 39–43 top, 56–7. Jane Miller 52 bottom. John Moss 67 bottom, 78, 80. Pictor Ltd 28. Picturepoint 59. Popperfoto 19, 35. Robert Harding Associates 37 bottom. Sally Anne Thompson 12 top, 16, 22, 23 top, 29 bottom, 30 top, 33 bottom, 46, 48 top left and bottom, 50 top right, 50 bottom, 51 bottom, 58, 62 top, 63, 65 bottom, 66, 67 top, 68 right, 70 top & bottom, 71, 74 bottom, 75 top, 77, 79, 81–3, 86, 87 top, 90, 92 top left, 94 top. Spectrum Colour Library 2–3, 10 top left. 10 bottom, 14, 21, 26, 37 top, 44 bottom, 49 top, 61, 74 top, 84, 94 bottom, 95. Stereoscopic Photography 38. Tony Stone Associates 72–3. ZEFA 8–9 (P Schoek), 11 (P Kornetzki), 36 (W L Hamilton), 45 (A Thau), 49 bottom (F Park), 53, 60 (M Gnade). Jacket front, Spectrum; Jacket back, ZEFA; endpapers Sally Anne Thompson.

Basset puppies enjoying a drink of water. Remember to protect your puppies against disease by having them vaccinated when they are 10 weeks old.